ST. PATRICK'S DAY

REVISED AND UPDATED

Dorothy Rhodes Freeman

Enslow Elementary

an imprint of

Enslow Publishers, Inc.

40 Industrial Road
Box 398
Berkeley Heights, NJ 07922
USA

http://www.enslow.com

Enslow Elementary, an imprint of Enslow Publishers, Inc.

Enslow Elementary® is a registered trademark of Enslow Publishers, Inc.

Library of Congress Cataloging-in-Publication Data

Freeman, Dorothy Rhodes.
   St. Patrick's Day / Dorothy Rhodes Freeman. — Rev. and updated.
      p. cm. — (Best holiday books)
   Summary: "Read about the history of St. Patrick, and find out why there is a
celebration for this saint"—Provided by publisher.
   Includes bibliographical references and index.
   ISBN-13: 978-0-7660-3046-6
   ISBN-10: 0-7660-3046-6
   1. Saint Patrick's Day—Juvenile literature. 2. Patrick, Saint, 373?–463?—Juvenile
literature. I. Title.
   GT4995.P3F74 2008
   394.262—dc22   2007002426

Printed in the United States of America

10 9 8 7 6 5 4 3 2 1

To Our Readers: We have done our best to make sure all Internet Addresses in this book were active and appropriate when we went to press. However, the author and the publisher have no control over and assume no liability for the material available on those Internet sites or on other Web sites they may link to. Any comments or suggestions can be sent by e-mail to comments@enslow.com or to the address on the back cover.

Every effort has been made to locate all copyright holders of material used in this book. If any errors or omissions have occurred, corrections will be made in future editions of this book.

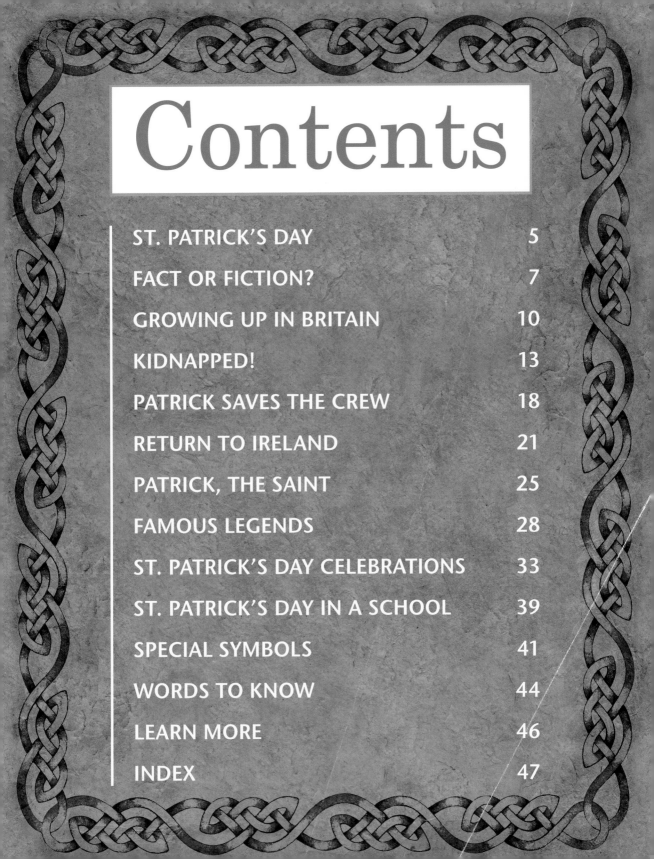

Contents

Traditional Irish dancers add a splash of color to New York City's 2006 St. Patrick's Day Parade.

ST. PATRICK'S DAY

ST. PATRICK'S DAY IS MARCH 17. THIS day is celebrated all over the world. People march in parades and marching bands play. Some sing Irish songs. Others dance Irish dances. Many people wear green because it is an Irish color. Corned beef and cabbage is a favorite meal on St. Patrick's Day. This day is a joyful time.

Saint Patrick is the patron saint of Ireland. In the Catholic Church, a saint is someone who is thought to be very special. A patron saint takes special care of a country or group. The Irish believe that Saint Patrick watches over them.

March 17 is believed to be the day of Patrick's death, around the year A.D. 460. That is more than fifteen hundred years ago. We are not certain of the exact date or year.

Corned beef and cabbage are traditional foods to serve on St. Patrick's Day.

FACT OR FICTION?

WE KNOW SOMETHING ABOUT SAINT Patrick from his own words. When he was an old man, he wrote about his life. He told how he came to Ireland. He described his life there. His writing has been saved for more than fifteen hundred years! In this book there are words in quotation marks. They are Patrick's own words.

St. Patrick's Basilica in Montreal, Canada, features this beautiful stained glass window. It includes many important symbols from St. Patrick's life.

Long ago, people learned about the past by listening to stories told by others. Sometimes those stories were true, and sometimes they were made up. When stories are told over and over again, they sometimes become legends. There are many legends about Saint Patrick.

It was a long time after Saint Patrick's death before men wrote down these stories. People study Saint Patrick's life. They debate about what is true. They wonder what was made up by the storytellers and writers. As you read about Saint Patrick, you can begin to decide what you think is true!

This is a page from the Book of Armagh. Some believe that St. Patrick owned the book, and may have written part of it.

GROWING UP
IN BRITAIN

PATRICK WAS BORN SOMEWHERE IN Britannia, which is now called Britain. Britain is an island that includes England, Scotland, and Wales. But Patrick was not British—or Irish. He was Roman.

A long time ago, much of Britain was ruled by the Roman Empire. Some Romans lived in Britain.

Patrick wrote that he lived by the sea in a large house. We think that he was wealthy because he wrote about servants in his house. Britain can be cold and damp. But Patrick's house may have been warm. Romans knew ways to keep a house warm. We know this because there are ruins of Roman houses in Britain.

Patrick wrote that he did not study when he was a boy. He did not believe in religion and prayer. He said he did not obey the priests. This was strange because Patrick's grandfather was a priest. His father also worked in the church. (Long ago, priests could marry and have children.)

The countries in orange, yellow, and blue were probably part of the Roman Empire at the time St. Patrick lived.

Forts were built to help protect people throughout the Roman Empire. These are the only remaining parts of a fort and wall that the ancient Romans built in England.

KIDNAPPED!

WHEN PATRICK WAS SIXTEEN, HIS life changed. He was kidnapped!

Across the sea was an island. It was called Hibernia. Now the sea is called the Irish Sea. The island is now called Ireland.

Some fierce men called raiders lived there. They sailed to other lands. They stole people from their homes and sold them as slaves.

The raiders were strong men. They would tie up people and carry them to their ships.

The raiders kidnapped Patrick. They also stole some of his family's servants.

The ship sailed to Ireland. There the raiders sold Patrick. Miliuc, an important chief, bought him. Patrick was a slave!

Miliuc owned herds of sheep. Patrick had to take care of them. He became a shepherd. He lived outdoors with the sheep. Like Britain, Ireland gets cold and wet. Patrick had no shelter. Perhaps he kept warm among the sheep.

Patrick had no one to talk to. He said he was among "barbarians," a word used to describe people one sees as uncivilized and cruel.

Patrick thought God was angry with him. He thought it was because he had not obeyed the priests. He began to pray. Sometimes he prayed all night.

Patrick wrote that he lived in the woods and on the mountains. We know shepherds take sheep

This map shows England and Ireland. When St. Patrick was alive, England was called Britannia and Ireland was called Hibernia.

SCOTLAND

IRELAND

ENGLAND

Atlantic Ocean

up to the mountains. The sheep graze there in warm weather and come down in the winter. Patrick said he prayed "through snow, through frost, through rain."

Six years passed. Patrick said prayers day and night. We do not know what he prayed for. Perhaps he asked for strength. Maybe he asked to go home.

One night, Patrick heard a voice. It told him that he would soon see his country.

It is believed that St. Patrick lived on Slemish Mountain (above) while he was a shepherd in Ireland.

St. Patrick heard a voice say that he would soon go home by ship. Here, an artist drew his version of the story.

Then the voice spoke again and said that Patrick's ship was ready.

Patrick was miles from the sea. Yet, the voice spoke about a ship! Patrick called the voice Victor. Maybe he thought that Victor was an angel.

Patrick ran away from Miliuc. He walked two hundred miles. He believed God was guiding him. Finally he reached the sea. There was a ship at the shore!

Patrick called to the ship's captain. He begged the captain to take him on board.

People who helped runaway slaves were punished. Perhaps the captain guessed that Patrick was a slave. The captain would not take Patrick on board.

Patrick could not go back to Miliuc. Slaves who ran away were killed. He started to leave. As he walked, he began to pray.

Suddenly, things changed. Patrick heard one of the ship's crew shouting to him to hurry on board the ship.

Patrick went on board. Some believe the ship had a cargo of Irish wolfhounds. These dogs were valued as hunters. They can fight a wolf and win. They can outrun a big elk. Wolfhounds were often shipped from Ireland to Britain. They were sold to wealthy men.

The ship set sail. The captain and crew treated Patrick well. If the ship went to Britain, Patrick might find his way home.

Some people believe that the ship that took St. Patrick away from Ireland had Irish wolfhounds on it.

PATRICK SAVES THE CREW

THE SHIP WAS BLOWN OFF ITS COURSE. It ran aground. The shore was rocky. The men and dogs had to get off the ship.

Patrick and the crew wandered for twenty-eight days. They did not see any people. They did not know where they were. Some think Patrick was in Britain. Others think he landed in a place called Gaul. Gaul is now the countries of France, Belgium, and part of Germany.

The land was deserted. There were no animals to hunt. The food supplies were gone. The men and the dogs were starving.

The captain grabbed Patrick and commanded him to pray to God to save them. Patrick told the captain to believe in God. He said God would send food.

Suddenly a herd of wild pigs appeared on the road. The men killed some of them. They ate the meat and got back their strength. The dogs had all they could eat, too. Later, the men found wild honey. They stayed at that place for two nights.

We are not sure what happened next, but Patrick wrote that he was captured again. He does not say who captured him.

One story says that wild-looking men captured the crew.

Wild pigs kept St. Patrick, the dogs, and the ship's crew from starving when they got off the ship.

This illustration from the 13th century shows St. Patrick asleep on a rock, with Christ watching over him.

They sold all but Patrick as slaves. Patrick watched the men. They hunted and fished. They gathered wild foods. Patrick remembered it all.

Another story says that Patrick was held captive by the captain. He wanted Patrick with him. He might need Patrick to pray for more food.

Both stories agree that the voice of Victor spoke to Patrick again. The voice said that Patrick would be with them for two months.

Two months passed. Patrick wrote: "The Lord delivered me out of their hands."

Patrick was free. He had seen what happened when he prayed. It is thought that he then became very religious. Patrick became a priest like his grandfather.

RETURN
TO IRELAND

YEARS PASSED. AT LAST, PATRICK found his way home. His mother and father welcomed their son. He had been gone so long.

Patrick then had a vision. In it, Victor handed Patrick a letter. Patrick read the first words. They said, "The voice of the Irish." Then Irish voices said, "Come walk among us once more."

Patrick's parents begged him not to leave. They said he had suffered so many

St. PATRICK of IRELAND

hardships. They said he should not go away again.

But Patrick was willing to return to Ireland. He left home. He didn't want to leave, but he thought God wanted him to go.

Patrick was made a bishop. Some priests went with him to Ireland.

Patrick's work was to start churches and encourage the Irish people to become Christians. That was sometimes hard to do. Most Irish people believed in spells and magic. They believed in many gods. Many people did not want to give up their beliefs.

St. Patrick had many churches built when he returned to Ireland, like this one to the left. Can you also see the one in the background of the stained glass window, above?

St. Patrick defeated the Druids. Many of them became priests.

Ireland was ruled by many chiefs. Some called them kings. They were like Miliuc, Patrick's former master. Each chief had advisers called Druids. The Druids led religious ceremonies as well as advising chiefs.

The Druids said they could see the future. They said that a stranger was coming. They said his teaching would end their way of life. Patrick was a stranger. He did teach another way of living. It is easy to see why the Druids were Patrick's enemies.

Celtic crosses combined the Irish people's old beliefs with Christianity.

Patrick's life was often in danger. Druids tried to kill him. Patrick said, "Daily I expect murder, fraud, or captivity." Some chiefs tried to kill Patrick. Once they chained him in irons for fourteen days.

Patrick faced the Druids. He convinced many chiefs to become Christians. He even made priests of some Druids. After this, many people became Christians. Patrick said he baptized thousands of Irish people.

This stone is located next to St. Patrick's Cathedral in Ireland.

NEAR HERE IS THE REPUTED SITE OF THE WELL WHERE ST. PATRICK BAPTISED MANY OF THE LOCAL INHABITANTS IN THE FIFTH CENTURY A.D

PATRICK, THE SAINT

SAINT PATRICK IS KNOWN AS THE patron saint of Ireland. The Irish believe that Saint Patrick watches over them.

Saint Patrick is often called the best-loved saint. People go to church to honor him. Even people who do not believe in religion celebrate his day. Why is he so loved and so popular?

Many people visit St. Patrick's Cathedral in New York City every day.

The answer is that he was a very loving person. He was kidnapped and sold. He was made a slave. But he did not become mean or bitter. He did not hate the raiders or Miliuc. When Patrick was an old man, he wrote, "I have mercy on the people who once took me captive."

Patrick could have had an easy life in Britain. Instead, he went back to Ireland. He wrote: "I came to the people of Ireland to give up my free birth for the benefit of others." We know Patrick cared about people and for the Irish.

Artists often show St. Patrick in bishop's robes.

FAMOUS
LEGENDS

STORYTELLERS TOLD MANY OTHER stories about Patrick. One legend tells about Patrick and the snakes of Ireland.

The legend says Patrick charmed all the snakes in Ireland. When he walked to the sea, all the snakes followed him. When they came to the sea, all the snakes swam away from Ireland. Ireland was rid of snakes forever.

On St. Patrick's Day people talk about the "wearing of the green." They may wear green clothing, or pin on a green ribbon. They wear green because of the legend of the shamrock.

Legend has it that Patrick was preaching about the Father, the Son, and the Holy Spirit. Patrick was telling people that all three made up one God. Some people questioned him. Why did Patrick say there was one God and worship three?

The legend says Patrick bent down. He picked a green shamrock. It was the leaf of a clover plant. He held it out, showing its leaf with three round parts. The three parts were all part of the same leaf. He compared the three parts that made one leaf of the shamrock to the three parts that made one God. The shamrock leaf became a symbol of Saint Patrick.

The Irish believe shamrocks

A St. Patrick's Day card from 1910 shows a man wearing green. People still wear green today for St. Patrick's Day.

The Wearing of the Green.

Shamrocks are often included in paintings and statues of St. Patrick.

bring good luck. They think shamrocks protect a person from evil spirits. Some Irish people who came to America carried shamrocks for good luck.

Another legend is about fairies and leprechauns (LEP-reh-kons). Irish people used to believe in magic spirits. Over time, the spirits became less important to the Irish. The spirits got smaller and became the "wee ones," or little people. These are the fairies.

It is said that fairies love to dance. They wear out a lot of shoes. Some of the wee ones are men dressed in green. These are the leprechauns. They carry a shoemaker's hammer and mend the fairies' shoes.

Leprechauns are said to be grouchy and mean. They prefer to live alone. Leprechauns work at night while the

The shamrock helped St. Patrick teach the people of Ireland about Christianity.

fairies sleep. The fairies pay the leprechauns with gold.

Leprechauns collect the pots of gold, which they hide. Legend says that if you catch one, he will lead you to his pot of gold. To find him, you can listen for the tap of his tiny hammer. But if you catch a leprechaun, do not take your eyes off of him. Otherwise, he will be gone in a second.

Patrick never saw a leprechaun, but the gentle saint might have smiled at the stories. Leprechauns do not look grouchy in pictures now. They usually look jolly. They may be dancing an Irish dance called a jig.

People believe that if you catch a leprechaun, you can demand his pot of gold.

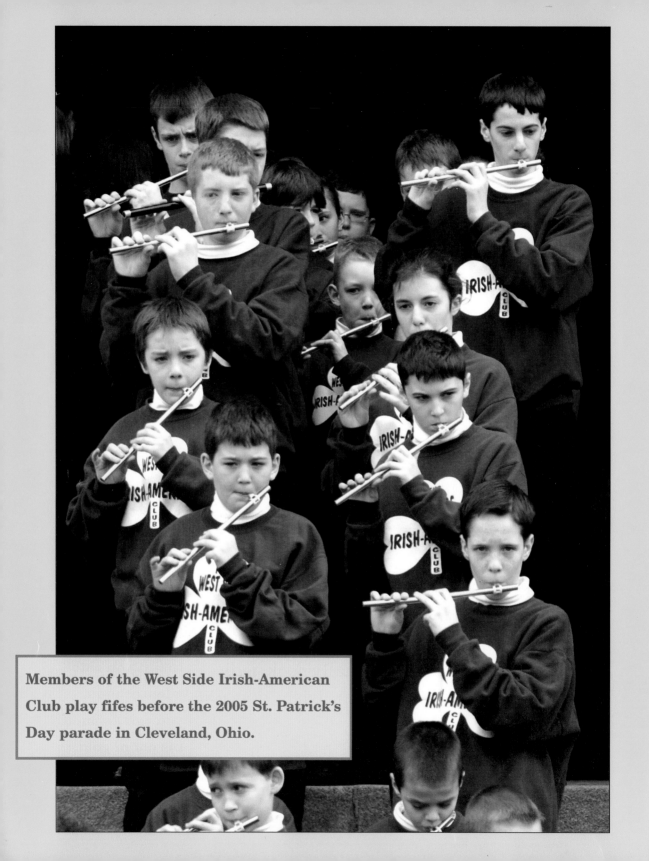

Members of the West Side Irish-American Club play fifes before the 2005 St. Patrick's Day parade in Cleveland, Ohio.

ST. PATRICK'S DAY CELEBRATIONS

ST. PATRICK'S DAY STARTED MANY years after Patrick died. Today, there are many ways people like to celebrate.

In Ireland, St. Patrick's Day is a holy day. Most people go to church. Then they spend time with family and friends. Sometimes they meet in a pub. A pub is like a restaurant and bar. They drink to Saint Patrick.

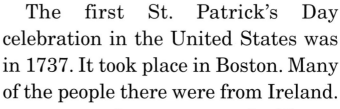

This person is dressed as St. Patrick for a parade in Denver, Colorado.

The first St. Patrick's Day celebration in the United States was in 1737. It took place in Boston. Many of the people there were from Ireland.

One way people like to celebrate St. Patrick's Day is to watch or march in parades. Thousands of people in towns and cities all over the world have parades on St. Patrick's Day. The parades began in New York City in the 1700s. The New York parade is still the longest.

There is also a big parade in Sydney, Australia. In Sydney, March 17 is nicknamed "Saint Paddy's Day." There are other St. Patrick's Day parades in cities in Canada, Africa, and South America. Even some of the cities in Ireland have

parades now. Sometimes marching bands from the United States go to Ireland to play in the parades.

Lots of people sing Irish songs on St. Patrick's Day. One of the most popular songs is called "When Irish Eyes Are Smilin'." Another is called "The Wearin' of the Green."

Some cities celebrate St. Patrick's Day by doing unusual things. In Chicago, some people color the water of the

Colorful costumes brighten up St. Patrick's Day parades in Ireland, too!

Chicago River green in honor of Saint Patrick. People in San Antonio, Texas, do the same thing with the San Antonio River.

In New York City, the Empire State Building lights the night sky with green lights for the holiday.

The town of Shamrock, Florida, was named after the shamrocks found in

Everyone comes out to see the Chicago River on St. Patrick's Day. It is dyed green!

St. Patrick's Cathedral on Madison Avenue in New York City is one of the most famous cathedrals named after him.

Ireland. Each St. Patrick's Day, many people send letters to be mailed from the post office there. That way, the postmark will say "Shamrock."

Even some businesses join in the celebration. Sometimes car washes give a free wash to green cars on St. Patrick's Day. Or a dry cleaner may clean green garments for free.

People also honor Saint Patrick by naming cathedrals for him. A cathedral is a large church. Famous ones that are named after Saint Patrick are in New York City and Dublin, Ireland.

These sisters are drawing shamrocks to decorate for St. Patrick's Day.

ST. PATRICK'S DAY IN A SCHOOL

ST. PATRICK'S DAY IS CELEBRATED in many schools. Children wear something green. Some wear all green clothing. Others pin on something green. It might be a ribbon or a shamrock.

In one school, students found small green footprints at the classroom door. They led into a cupboard. Maybe a leprechaun could be found inside! The children hunted for the leprechaun who had left the tracks.

In the cupboard, they found only a tiny shoe and cookies. The cookies were shaped like shamrocks. The children ate the cookies. They made leprechauns from green paper. Their teacher told them about Saint Patrick. Then she taught them an Irish dance and an Irish song.

Cookies like these are popular on St. Patrick's Day!

SPECIAL SYMBOLS

A SYMBOL IS SOMETHING THAT stands for another thing. The shamrock is a symbol for Saint Patrick.

Flags are symbols for countries. The Irish flag has three stripes. The stripes run side by side. The stripe on the left is green. It is for the people of southern Ireland. The stripe on the right is orange. It is for the people of Northern Ireland.

The girl in this 1908 drawing is holding a special Irish flag.

For many years, the Irish of the south and north have been fighting. The middle stripe of the flag is white. It stands for hope that the two parts of Ireland will stop fighting. It is a hope for peace.

There is another Irish flag. It is not the official flag. It has a green background. In the center is a golden Irish harp.

The Irish harp is another symbol of Ireland. A harp is a musical instrument with strings to pluck. Long ago, the harp was played while storytellers told tales.

This is the official Irish flag.

The harps were small. They had a sweet tone. Some harps were decorated with shamrocks.

If Patrick were alive now, he might enjoy a parade. Perhaps he would eat corned beef and cabbage. He might join in singing Irish songs while the harpist played. What do you enjoy doing for St. Patrick's Day?

Music is an important part of St. Patrick's Day celebrations. People play traditional instruments and sing favorite Irish songs.

WORDS TO KNOW

bishop—A rank above a priest in some Christian churches.

Britannia—The ancient name for the island that now includes England, Scotland, and Wales.

captivity—Being a prisoner or a slave.

cathedral—A very large church.

Druids—Men who advised the Irish chiefs.

Gaul—The European nation that is now the countries of France, Belgium, and part of Germany.

Hibernia—The ancient name for Ireland.

Ireland—An island country west of Britain.

irons—Iron bands fastened around the ankle or wrist of a prisoner or slave.

legend—A story that was told over and over before it was written down. A legend may or may not be true.

leprechaun—An elf resembling a little old man, thought to own hidden gold.

patron saint—A saint believed to take special care of a country or group.

priest—A minister in some Christian churches.

Romans—People from the old empire of Rome.

saint—A holy person who has died and is honored by the church for his or her good life. The abbreviation for saint is "St."

St. Patrick's Day—March 17, the day that is celebrated in Saint Patrick's honor.

shamrock—A type of clover plant with a three-part leaf.

symbol—A thing that stands for a person, place, or idea.

LEARN MORE

Books

Roop, Peter and Connie Roop. *Let's Celebrate St. Patrick's Day*. Millbrook, Conn.: Millbrook Press, 2003.

Carmen Bredeson. *St. Patrick's Day*. New York: Children's Press, 2003.

Rosinsky, Natalie M. *St. Patrick's Day*. Minneapolis: Compass Point Books, 2002.

Internet Addresses

Holiday Fun: St. Patrick's Day
http://www.primarygames.com/holidays/st.patricksday/
stpatricksday.htm

St. Patrick's Day
http://www.kidsdomain.com/holiday/patrick/

St. Patrick's Day Crafts and Activities
http://www.enchantedlearning.com/crafts/stpatrick/

INDEX

parents, 11, 21–22
priesthood, 22
sainthood, 6, 25, 27
shipwrecked, 18–20
slavery, 14–16
voices in dreams,
15–16, 20, 21
prayers, 15, 16–17, 19

R

Romans, 10, 11

S

St. Patrick's Day
celebrations of,
33–37
classroom activities,
39–40

in Ireland, 33, 34–35
in New York, 34,
36
parades, 34–35
shamrock, 29–30, 39,
40, 41, 43
Shamrock, Florida,
36–37
snakes, 28
South America, 34

V

Victor, 16, 20, 21

W

"wearing of the
green," 29